APRIL 2022

AN ANTHOLOGY OF ARTICLES

BRAIN BOOSTER ARTICLES

Contents

Preface

"Start writing, no matter what. The water does not flow until the faucet is turned on".

-Louis L'Amour

This book is a bouquet of articles contributed by students, professors and academicians. Hundreds of students and professors are contributing their work to Brain Booster Articles, we are here to provide ample information about Law and Contemporary issues. Our aim is to provide a platform for today's generation to express their views and ideas on law and contemporary law.

CORPORATE SOCIAL RESPONSIBILITY: A CONCEPT OF HUMAN RIGHTS RESPONSIBILITY OF BUSINESS ENTITIES

Author: Monalisa Chandra, PhD Scholar from NLUJA Assam

This context has given an exploratory concept in terms a trade-related, market-friendly pattern of human rights in comparison to the pattern with general Human rights that has been placed in the general Declaration of Human Rights (UDHR) [1]. It gives all attention on the act of the UDHR in relation with the body ruling business ethics and specifically looks to offer certain norms on the responsibilities of transnational business companies and other Business undertakings. These norms are conceptualized into basic ideas: the intertextuality of the norms; the network idea of trade and business acts and behaviour; and the categories of business rights and obligation. The United Nations Commission on Human Rights, particularly the Sub-Commission provides the important sites of critique and renewal. The transmitted to Human Rights Commission norms are open to further consideration and receivable of feedback by April 2005 and have been proposed in the interest of business and trade ,along with Human Rights NGOs and such social activism have already began to deploy such norms owing to human rights strategy. There is a form of zero tolerance in business practices and conduct enshrined so as the human rights violations are avoided. The main single minded approach of such developments of norms is only for benefit of future of globalization.

There are basically two types of international laws i.e. the hard law and the soft law which are referred as human rights texts since there cannot be a lone derivative for the new norms. There lies the problem of legal legitimacy along with the communal legitimating human rights responsibility bearers. If there a too little spell of prior texts which can weaken the instruments of human rights then such recourse makes itself defeating. Since various norms have various senders and receivers those promote and protect the human rights. The greater the reference of hard and soft laws the greater is the crises of action based understanding of human rights and none can reality check these remains of conductive human rights. No reflexive student can remain innocent of such patterns of normative hybridism. Not only the bodies of human rights and social moments but also the activists can measure justice. The old references are accent to new norms also the encyclopaedic references do complicate the understanding of these new forms of 'illiteracy of the literate'. The greater the political economy in self-preferentiality, the greater production of contemporary human rights [2].

Every business ethic should remain subjected to the disciplinary regimes of human rights whether it is based on civil, cultural, economic, political and social rights as adopted by the United Nation systems. The Business Enterprises are defined by Article 21, that includes Business entity both domestic and international sphere including transnational corporation, contractors, suppliers, partnership or legal firms. All norms shall be applied to these business enterprises as per their matter of practice thereby forbidding the violation of human rights. These norms are not only applicable to larger business but also to local business that include bakeries, dry cleaners etc

Article 1, state about the primary state responsibility where all the macro and micro activities of any business conduct are extended as a state responsibility. Their main aim is to 'promote, secure, respect and ensure protection of human rights as recognized in nation as well as international specifically to the business enterprises and transnational corporate and these organisation need to fulfil these obligations in respect to activity and influence since State is unaware of such activities beforehand and these form of responsibilities are no where specified. The states have a non negotiable duty to translate these norms into legislations.

The Business Entities also must inform themselves about the impact of their activities on the firstly the human rights violation and the human abuses. Human abuse have a direct impact on the victim like slave-like labour practice, unconscious forms of child labour, sexual harassment at work place, rape, etc. The human rights hostile business includes the attempts to harass the NGOs, Capture and control of human rights markets etc.

Example: A well known MNC that has its primary work location in India and has extended its branches to some other parts of the countries. It has around more than 20,000 employees working out of which only 4000 are female employees. There are also cases of "sexual harassment at workplace" thereby violation of human rights of female employees at workplace. The same is the reason for the low number of female employees in such companies that is yet another violation as seen by the NGOs that might try to emphasize these important issues to the state with the help of activists and try to stop such violation with those obligatory norms those have been laid down. The state shall discuss with all the five member committee of the activists of NGOs and will come to common norms and deploy zero tolerance in such acts. Try to either remove the practices or reform the ideologies with the help of state.

There are various other examples of such activism like for Bhopal Gas tragedy , there was a violation of norms by the UNION CARBIDE CORPORATION, the transnational organization that was involved in violating had to face the effective criticism so as the entity was forced to be closed for the greater benefit of the people living around. But still the compensations remain pending to all affected people on grounds of violation of business conduct and can only be achieved with the help of the state.

So it is important for these business entities to follow the obligations keeping in mind the human rights which may be articulated in norms or as mandatory duties. Article 3 encodes the responsibilities of business entities so as it forbids them to benefit themselves from war crimes, crimes against humanity, genocide, torture, forced labour etc. other violations of international laws. These codes will be beneficial for the expansion of social and economical opportunities of particularly the developing countries.

Article 10 is the final and the third obligatory articulation that promotes 'transparency, accountability and prohibition of corruption.

<u>IMPORTANT EXTRACTS</u>

- "Contestation is inevitable, as are future compromises. What makes the Norms, and the Commentary, precious is the now-proclaimed zero tolerance for egregious forms of business conduct and practices that transgress human rights and constantly reproduce human rights violations. This single-minded pursuit of a human rights-oriented future for globalisation and human development is perhaps the only pertinent way ahead" [3].
- "Exuberant intertextuality of norms thus partly reflects the endless 'turf' wars within the United Nations system. Besides the problem of internal (within United Nations) legitimacy, the optimality question also relates to legitimating with the communities of the eventual bearers of human rights responsibilities"[4].
- The human rights responsibility of business entities may be summated in terms of duties of non-benefit from human rights violations; duties of influence; and duties of implementation. State responsibility is unqualified; transnational corporations and other business enterprises bear these responsibilities only 'within their respective spheres of activity and influence' [5].

CHAPTER TWO

COLLECTIVE BARGAINING IN INDIA

Author: Tanay Bansal, III year of B.A.,LL.B.(Hons.) from UPES Dehradun

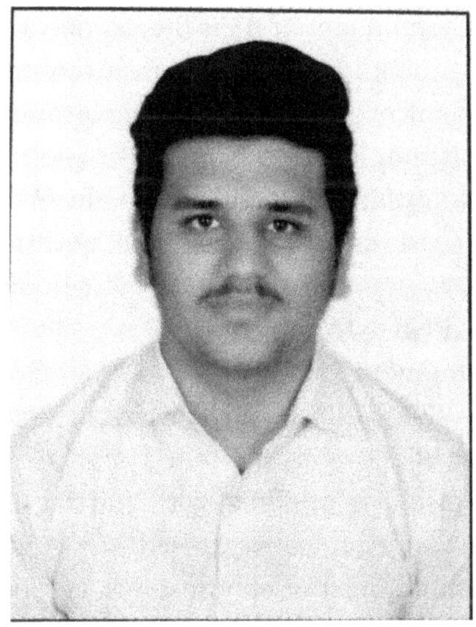

INTRODUCTION

Peace is required for progress, because disputes waste the society's valuable time, effort, and money. But, in reality, confrontation is unavoidable. Commerce, business, development work, administration, and so on all suffer as a result of the lengthy process of settling disputes through traditional courts of law. There are alternate ways of industrial dispute resolution, including as collective bargaining, conciliation[1], mediation, arbitration, worker engagement in management, wage boards, and so on, to get out of this maze of litigation. Collective bargaining is regarded as the greatest option available since it allows disputants to sit down together and address their disagreements in an amiable and respectful manner.Several theories, including those from industrial relations, economics, political science, history, and sociology, as well as writings by activists, workers, and labour groups, have attempted to define and explain collective bargaining. According to one theory, collective bargaining is a human right that deserves legal protection.The Supreme Court of Canada thoroughly analysed the reasons for recognising collective bargaining to be a human right in Facilities Subsector Bargaining Assn. v. British Columbia in June 2007. In this case, the Court made the following observations:

1. The freedom to collectively bargain with an employer increases workers' human dignity, liberty, and autonomy by allowing them to influence the formation of workplace regulations and therefore obtain some control over a major component of their life, namely their employment.

2. Collective bargaining is more than just a tool for achieving external goals...rather, it is organically useful as a self-government experience.

3. Collective bargaining enables workers to attain a sort of workplace democracy while also ensuring the rule of law in the workplace. Workers get a voice to influence the creation of rules that govern a significant portion of their lives.

<u>COLLECTIVE BARGAINING IN INDIA</u>

Origin and Development

Because Collective Bargaining is an offshoot of Trade Union action, it is necessary to first trace the origins of Trade Union activity. N.M. Lokhande, a factory worker himself, is credited with starting the organised labour movement in India. In 1884, he organised an agitation in Bombay and wrote a memorandum asking a weekly rest day, compensation for injuries, and other requests, and in response to these demands, the mill owners of Bombay gave a weekly holiday. In fact, the Bombay Mill Hands' Association was formed in 1890, with Lokhande as chairman, and the workers' journal "Deenabandhu" was launched.The trade union movement gained traction at the end of World War I, and the years 1918-21 were watershed moments in the history of the Indian labour movement. The Madras Labour Union, founded by P.P. Wadia in 1918, was India's first trade union37. By 1920, practically every sector of the Indian economy had a trade union to represent the legitimate interests of the working masses. Collective bargaining formally began in the 1920s in Ahmedabad's textile sector, around the time Mahatma Gandhi introduced the notion of arbitration. Collective bargaining began as a result of the failure of arbitration. Following that, a slew of collective bargaining agreements were put in place, particularly following the country's independence[2].However, because neither British India nor Independent India provided legal procedures for collective bargaining, there was little support for its expansion. Nonetheless, as in many other nations, numerous statutory mechanisms aided collective bargaining in India. The Trade Union Act of 1929, the Bombay Industrial Relations Act of 1946, the Industrial Disputes Act of 1947, and the Madhya Pradesh Industrial Relations Act of 1960 established a consultation mechanism and cleared the path for collective bargaining.

Validity & Recognition

1. Industrial Disputes Act, 1947 –The Act was primarily established to provide a forum for dispute resolution. Section 18 of the Act states that "a settlement reached by agreement between the employer and the worker other than in the course of a conciliation action shall be binding on the parties to the agreement..." Thus, any settlement other than conciliation that may occur as a result of a contractual agreement between the employer and the employee is nothing more than an implication of the collective bargaining agreement. Section 18, in other terms, recognises collective bargaining. In reality, the Act's definition of settlement includes the element of collective bargaining.

The examination of the salient provisions of the Act in the case of Workmen of Dimakuchi Tea Estate vs. The Management of Dimakuchi Tea Estate reveals that the primary objects of the Act are – "(1) the promotion of measures for securing and preserving amity and good relations between the employer and workmen; (2) an investigation and settlement of industrial disputes, between employers and employers, employers and workmen, or workmen and workmen, with a right of reprise.

2. Trade Union Act, 1926 –The Act provides for the registration of trade unions and establishes the union's rights, obligations, and immunities. The primary reason for the formation of a trade union is to govern the relationship between the employer and the employee or between themselves, and it is well documented that collective bargaining is one method of regulating such a relationship.

The court recognises collective bargaining in the case of D.N. Banerjee vs. P.R. Mukherjee. According to Justice Chandra Shekhar Aiyer, "having regard to the modern condition of society in which capital and labour have organised themselves into groups for the purpose of fighting and settling their disputes on the basis of the theory that Union is Strength, collective bargaining has come to stay."

3. The Industrial Employment (Standing Orders) Act, 1946- The employer creates a standing order that outlines the terms of employment. According to Section 3 of the Act, the employer must first submit a draught standing order to the Certifying Officer, which should be as close to the model standing order as practicable. Following that, the said Officer shall forward a copy of the draught to the trade union or to the workmen, if there is no trade union, for objections (if any), and after giving both parties an opportunity to be heard, the Officer shall certify the standing order with necessary modifications (if any) and shall send copies to both parties.

Thus, the process of creating a standing order plainly indicates that both the employer and the employee participate in it, rather than it being in the hands and whims of either of them, albeit with the assistance of the Certifying Officer who works as a negotiator. In other words, drafting a standing order is a form of negotiation with the assistance of a third party (the Certifying Officer), and it involves the collective bargaining process. In the case of Glaxo Laboratories. Labour Court Justice Desai assesses the Act's impending need: "In the days of laissez-faire, when industrial relations were governed by the harsh and weighted law of hire and fire, the management was the supreme master, the relationship being referable to a contract between unequals and the action of the management treated almost sacrosanct." As the long title suggests, the Act obliged employers in industrial facilities to specify with sufficient precision the terms of employment under them and to make those circumstances known to the workers employed by them. The contract was imposed by statute rather than negotiated by two unequal parties."

4. The Constitution of India —The validity of collective bargaining is justified in the Indian Constitution's Chapters on Fundamental Rights and Directive Principles of State Policy. In this context, Article 19 allows for the formation of associations, which calls into question the validity of trade unions, and as previously said, one of the primary goals of trade unions is collective bargaining. Furthermore, various Directive Principles justify rules for improving labour conditions in general, and Article 43-A in specifically states that the State shall ensure worker engagement in management. Although the aforementioned Directives are not immediately enforceable in a court of law, their binding nature can be demonstrated with the help of

various Apex Court of India judgements.

In the case of Re Kerala Education Bill[3], the Supreme Court stated that, while directive principles cannot override fundamental rights, the court should use "the principles of harmonious construction and should attempt to give effect to both as much as possible" in determining the scope and ambit of fundamental rights.

RECOGNITION

The readiness of an employer or an employers' association to bargain with a certain union is referred to as the union's "recognition". Thus, recognition is the process through which management recognises and accepts a trade union as representing some or all of the workers in an enterprise or industry and agrees to hold negotiations on any matters affecting those workers. When this acceptance includes the management's readiness to bargain with that union or unions, they are referred to as a negotiating agent or agents. The National Commission on Labour placed a high value on the issue of union recognition.The provision for union recognition has been realised, according to the Commission, as evidenced by the...Bombay Industrial Relations Act, 1946 and certain other state Acts (Madhya Pradesh and Rajasthan), the amendments incorporated (but not enforced) in the Trade Union Act and the Code of Discipline, and the fact that it was included in the Second Plan. The Commission proposed that all enterprises employing 100 or more workers or investing more than a certain amount of capital be required to recognise the union under a Central Law. The Commission also advocated for the rights of recognised unions. Nonetheless, there is no national law requiring trade unions to be recognised.However, other states have enacted legal provisions for recognition, including Maharashtra, Andhra Pradesh, Madhya Pradesh, West Bengal, and Orissa. Thus, notwithstanding the absence of expressly centrally mandated regulations on collective bargaining in India, there are sufficient safeguards to ensure the relevance of collective bargaining in India.

CONCLUSION

Collective bargaining is a process of making common decisions that essentially symbolises a democratic way of life in the workplace. For collective bargaining to be successful, the process must begin with proposals rather than demands, and the participants must be ready and willing to compromise; otherwise, the entire concept of collective bargaining would be frustrated. The problem in the Indian context is that the absence of any statutory provisions at the Central Level for the recognition of a representative trade union by an employer impacts the trade union's bargaining strength. Aside from the fact that unorganised labour is a barrier, unions are often weak.Rivalry based on caste, creed, and religion is another feature of Indian Trade Unions that impedes good collective bargaining. Furthermore, split of unions based on political views and a poor financial situation stifle the growth of Trade Unions.

As a result, it is advised that India provide for trade union recognition at the central level in order to maintain peace and harmony among management and workers, which in turn can provide better service to the community and thus lead to economic growth and progress. In fact, India is required by international law to establish an effective process for collective bargaining. In this regard, it is also suggested that India ratify ILO Conventions No. 87 of 1948 and No. 98 of 1949, which both guarantee the right to effective collective bargaining. In a nutshell, we might say that the time has arrived to repeat history.According to Sir Henry Maine, a progressive society shifts from status to contract. However, given the importance of collective bargaining as an effective tool for the resolution of industrial disputes, the progressive society must go in the other direction, i.e. from contract to status rather than status to contract.

CHAPTER THREE

COVID19 AND ITS EFFECT ON FUNDAMENTAL RIGHTS

Author: Rahul Sharma, Assistant professor from Vivekananda college of Law, Aligarh

INTRODUCTION

The World Health Organization has labelled the Coronavirus illness (also known as COVID-19) a pandemic, which has broken countries throughout the world, destabilised people's living standards, and disturbed global businesses. More than 248 thousand people have died as a result of it over the world.[i]This sickness was initially found in the Chinese city of Wuhan and has since spread to nearly every country on the planet, including India. Since COVID-19 was discovered in India, the Indian government has taken a number of preventative precautions. The Indian government imposed a nationwide lockdown on March 24, 2020, as a precautionary step to prevent the sickness from spreading.

The lockdown was first imposed for 21 days, but it was subsequently prolonged for another 14 days by the government, and it was recently extended for another 14 days by the government. The key question raised by politicians, academics, intellectuals, significant figures, and the general public is: 'Was the lockdown imposed legitimately, or is it infringing on citizens' fundamental rights?"A catastrophe is a sudden, catastrophic occurrence that severely disrupts a community's or society's functioning and results in human, material, economic, or environmental losses that surpass the community's or society's ability to cope utilising its resources".[ii]

COVID-19, according to the above description, is a disaster since there are no vaccinations or drugs available to help battle the illness, and it has caused the country's functioning to be interrupted.According to "section 6 of the Disaster Management Act, the government can take" whatever step it deems appropriate for catastrophe prevention, mitigation, preparedness, and capacity building in the case of a dangerous disaster scenario or disaster[iii]. The national government, according to "section 35 of the Disaster Management Act", has the authority to take whatever action it considers appropriate for disaster relief.[iv]

<u>LOCKDOWN – A VIOLATION OF FUNDAMENTAL RIGHTS</u>

COVID-19 is a coronavirus-related illness that originated in China. On December 31, 2019, this new coronavirus was initially found in Wuhan, "China's Hubei province's largest city, and was first reported to the WHO Country Office in China and the WHO labelled the COVID-19 outbreak a worldwide health emergency on January 30, 2020". The global coronavirus pandemic has caused death, damage, and turmoil, and COVID-19's breakout has "brought social and economic life to a halt".To tackle the sickness, the Indian government implemented a total "lockdown in most parts of the 22 states and union territories where confirmed cases had been detected" in the last week of March 2020. Since then, the Indian government has declared victory in the coronavirus epidemic, claiming "that the number of cases would have been higher if the statewide lockdown had not been enacted". "However, given the recent increase of COVID-19 positive cases" and the state of the economy, we are less likely to embrace this explanation of success.

On "Prime Minister Shri Narendra Modi's request, India conducted a 14-hour voluntary public curfew" on March 22,2020. From March 24, 2020, there was a 21-day national lockdown. Following PM Modi's declaration on March 24, 2020, the Centre justified the pan-India lockdown by citing "lack of consistency in measures implemented by states as well as their execution." "The National Disaster Management Authority (NDMA) used its powers under section 6(2)(i) of the Disaster Management Act, 2005", to impose the lockdown.[v]

India prolonged the statewide lockdown to May 3 2020 on April 14, 2020, "followed by two-week extensions on May 3 and 17 with significant relaxations". The government began "unlocking the country in three phases" beginning June 1 (barring "containment zones").The global coronavirus pandemic has caused death, damage, and turmoil, and COVID-19's breakout has "brought social and economic life" to a halt. To tackle the sickness, "the Indian government implemented a total lockdown in most parts of the 22 states and union territories where confirmed cases had been detected" in the last week of March 2020. Since then, the Indian government has declared victory in the coronavirus epidemic, claiming "that the number of cases would have been higher if the statewide lockdown had not been" enacted.However, given the "recent increase of COVID-19 positive cases" and the state of the economy, we are less likely to embrace this explanation of success.[vi]

On "Prime Minister Shri Narendra Modi's request, India conducted a 14-hour voluntary public curfew" on March 22. From March 24, 2020, there was a 21-day national lockdown. "Following PM Modi's declaration on March 24, 2020", the Centre justified the pan-India lockdown by citing "lack of consistency in measures implemented by states as well as their execution." "The National Disaster Management Authority (NDMA) used its powers under section 6(2)(i) of the Disaster Management Act, 2005", to impose the lockdown.

India prolonged the statewide lockdown to May 3 2020 on April 14, 2020, "followed by two-week extensions on May 3 and 17 with significant relaxations". The "government began unlocking the country in three phases" beginning June 1 (barring "containment zones"). A lockdown is an all-encompassing edict that restricts a variety of civil freedoms.The first tier of restrictions in a lockdown are "freedom of mobility, freedom to practise one's chosen profession, trade, or occupation, and freedom to dwell in any region of the country". The second layer of restrictions is the result of instances of excess when enforcing the first, resulting in a blatant "infringement of the otherwise anonymous right to life and personal liberty".

"The fact that the state's capacity to order a lockdown and people' rights to reject excessive limitations on their civil freedoms are both born out of the same constitution, the holy text,in the words of Justice Rohinton Nariman, makes this examination" of lockdown critical. As a result, the examination is governed by the Indian Constitution.

It's worth noting that the National Disaster Management Act of 2005 established restrictions restricting freedom of commerce, activity, and profession. Notably, these standards do not impose any restrictions on one's ability to roam freely. Citizens' freedom of movement is "restricted through a network of executive orders issued under Section 144 of the Code of Criminal Procedure, 1973", in conjunction with the Home Ministry's addition and the colonial-era Epidemic Diseases Act.

Any individual "who is deprived of his right to livelihood" without following the law's reasonable and "fair procedure can dispute the deprivation" as a violation of Article 21's right to life. One would suppose that when the Government of India announced a national lockdown under the Disaster Management Act 2005 "to halt the spread of COVID-19, they felt obligated, under Olga Tellis' settled law, to pay individuals whose livelihoods would be harmed by the lockdown".

Thousands of individuals, however, were bereft of their livelihood virtually overnight, with no notice, choice, or warning. Many people who worked for a daily salary became "homeless and hungry", and they began wandering back to their town. Others who were worried about their paychecks at the end of the month joined the lengthy march to safety. This mass evacuation of employees to their villages prompted state governments to issue orders "to provide them with food and shelter, but no certainty of compensation" was offered. When petitioned, the "Supreme Court" chose to reject the case, stating imperiously that "if food was given, what need did people have for a wage?"

"With all humility, such dismissal appears to disregard the law established by a Constitutional Bench of the Supreme Court in Olga Tellis, which states that any person who is deprived of his right to livelihood except in accordance with a just and fair procedure established by law can challenge the deprivation as violating the right to life conferred by Article 21".

The Court was required to determine "whether citizens had been deprived of their livelihood in a just and fair manner and whether the state was required under Article 21 of the Indian Constitution to pay citizens a compensatory minimum wage if they were deprived of such livelihood as a result of directions under the Disaster Management Act, 2005".

Not only did the Court fail to scrutinize the scope of power under the Disaster Management Act to ensure that it did not go beyond the mandate of Article 21, but it also failed to investigate whether the law-enforced procedure under the Industrial Disputes Act was being followed by workers in both organised and unorganised industries.

"Article 21, which is a fundamental right, includes the right to privacy as part of the right to life". However, in the public interest, the exercise of such a right may be limited.[vii]"In the case of Justice K.S Puttaswamy v Union of India[viii], the Supreme Court decided that the right to privacy is a fundamental right under Article 21 of the Constitution, and established the following criteria" to determine whether the State's limits on the exercise of this right are reasonable:

1. The activity must be supported by legal authority.

2. The activity must be motivated by a reasonable goal.

3. A proper balance must be struck "between the restrictions imposed and the necessity for them".

4. The "existence of procedural safeguards against exploitation of the limitation".[ix]

The installation of limitation on the above-mentioned criterion must be examined in the current COVID-19 circumstance. The second requirement is met since a reasonable goal of the action is to protect public health and life. The Epidemic Diseases Act of 1987 establishes "a legal basis for the action done, so passing the first criteria". "There is also a healthy balance between" the necessity for and the state's interference with basic rights. The only omission appears to be in the "case of the last argument".The aforementioned Act "neither defines the word dangerous epidemic sickness nor provides any safeguards against the abuse of the powers granted" to the government. It also protects state personnel who carry out their duties under the Act from legal prosecution, thereby opening the door to misuse of the power granted by the Act. As a result, the Act does not appear to pass the Puttaswamy reasonableness test.

CONSTITUTIONAL VALIDITY OF COVID 19 LOCKDOWN?

Another question is if there were any other options besides enforcing a lockdown: Could the government have declared an emergency and seized complete control of the situation "under the powers granted by Article 352 of the Indian Constitution"?The answer to this question is a resounding 'no.' "The government could not have used article 352 of the Constitution because it no longer includes the term internal disturbance,which was a broad term that covered a variety of activities before the 44th Amendment to the Indian Constitution amended it and limited its applicability to situations of national security caused by war, external aggression, or armed rebellion". "People are protesting the lockdown restrictions" in some parts of the country.Rather of following the regulations, "such as social separation", they have repeatedly broken them and questioned "the government's choice to enforce the lockdown". They appear to be "arguing that the lockdown is infringing on their human rights because they are unable to move and function freely", as guaranteed by Article 19 of the constitution.[x]

Part III of the Indian constitution covers fundamental rights. While it is accurate that everyone should have the freedom to express their rights without fear of retaliation, none of the articles or legislation can be considered absolute since exceptions exist in unusual circumstances.This argument was made by the "Supreme Court in the case Re: Noise Pollution v Unknown[xi], when the Court emphasised that while free speech and the right to express oneself are essential rights, they are not absolute".[xii]Furthermore, when an individual exercises his or her basic rights, he or she should do so in a way that does not damage others. "Demonstrations are also a manner of expression of the rights provided under article 19(1)(a)" according to the Supreme Court.[xiii]Demonstrations, whether political, religious, social, or other, that cause "public disturbances or act as nuisances, or cause or threaten to cause some actual public or private injury, are not protected under article 19(1)(a)".

As a result, based on the Supreme Court's decisions, "we can deduce that mass gatherings and protests" by a small segment of the population may cause significant inconvenience and may increase the risk of the "deadly disease spreading to other parts of the population", endangering the lives of others, thereby constituting a "violation of Article 21 of the Constitution, which protects" the lives of others.[xiv]It's also important to remember what a citizen's basic responsibilities are. Article 51-A states that every citizen is responsible for upholding and protecting India's sovereignty, unity, and integrity, as well as promoting harmony and fraternity.[xv]

In Javed v State of Haryana[xvi], it was ruled, "Fundamental rightsshould not be read in isolation", according to the court. They must be examined with the chapter on state policy directive principles and article 51A fundamental duties.

The court ruled in a daily decision in the case The Registrar High Court v The State of Maharashtra[xvii]"that while the court expects appropriate actions from the State authorities, it also expects individuals to remind themselves of their basic responsibilities" in dealing with the COVID-19 pandemic epidemic. As a result, when certain groups of individuals ignore the lockdown and walk to the streets in large numbers to carry out their own functions, they are breaking the Constitution's essential fundamental obligations.They are not only breaching the laws when they meet in large groups, but they are also preparing the path for the sickness to spread. Others in their immediate vicinity will suffer as a result of this. We're all familiar with the necessity doctrine, which states that "necessity knows no law."

LEGALITY OF NATIONAL "HOUSE-ARREST"

The Janata Curfew was announced four days in advance, but the millions of Indians who needed to organise their lives and enterprises received just four hours' warning. Heartbreaking scenes "at railway stations, interstate bus terminals, state crossings, labour markets, and other areas where scores of people have been forced to work" while separated from their families have been captured as part of the chaotic aftermath of the statewide lockdown.Even if an emergency is technically declared, the right to life cannot be taken away as a result of the Janata government's modification. The emergency measures have not even been triggered in this situation. If the government can circumvent the Constitution's emergency provisions and take such drastic measures with widespread support, one might wonder if such provisions – which not only specify how fundamental rights can be suspended but also lay out the constitutional-legislative oversight over such suspension – are now completely meaningless.

Isn't this a death sentence for daily bettors, street vendors, migratory workers, and small company owners? Clauses (a) and (e) of Article 39 demand that the government make every effort to ensure that people have a right to adequate means of subsistence and that people are not forced to work in jobs that are inappropriate for them due to economic necessities.These responsibilities are "part of the country's Directive Principles of State Policy", which are seen as essential to the country's government. The current state of emergency would generate situations that would be in violation of these commitments. COVID-19 vs. economic death is a difficult decision. For whatever reason, the citizen has been stripped of his or her rights.For whatever good reason, the citizen has been stripped of her right to choose.[xviii]Returning to the original point, is a "lock-down" constitutionally acceptable in the absence of a state of "emergency, and therefore with freedom of movement and right to livelihood intact"?[xix]

The "doctrine of necessity is a common law doctrine" that is used to help people get through tough situations.[xx]The law does not regard a vacuum, thus rather than allowing the problem to escalate, a solution must be sought.[xxi]As a result, the government used the "principle of necessity to impose the Lockdown as the only way to stop" COVID-19 from spreading.Furthermore, the constitution's article 31-B states that some actions have the power to override "basic rights, and that these actions cannot be declared unconstitutional on that basis". The people' fundamental rights are not violated as a result of the lockdown.

Despite the fact that certain actions are prohibited, the government supports the provision of essential items, which are a person's fundamental needs. Furthermore, the government gives "food and relief items to the less fortunate members of society". "All medical facilities are available, and government authorities are always" willing to assist people who require assistance.The government has recently set up special trains and buses to carry migrant workers "back to their homes". It has effectively optimised"the use of technology in both the private and public sectors to allow work from home", as well as in schools and colleges for online education.

As a result, the central government's lockdown is legal and has a connection to the shared goal of preventing "the spread of COVID-19 by preserving social distance norms. People's arguments against the lockdown, which emphasise violations of fundamental rights", lack coherence.As a result, "no fundamental rights have been infringed upon or jeopardized". Many nations, like the United States and the United Kingdom, have praised "India's efforts in combating COVID-19, and it is critical that we, as citizens, acknowledge the steps and fight against the epidemic as well". As a result, it is critical that in a difficult and disastrous scenario, everyone comes together, stands together, follows the measures, and successfully overcomes the issue.

FUNDAMENTAL FREEDOM AND PROPORTIONALITY OF RESTRICTION DURING COVID-19

The phrase "extraordinary times call for exceptional measures" is frequently used to explain actions that elicit reflective responses from citizens. There is no denying that in emergent conditions, measurements must also be emergent, and properlyso.However, a line between extraordinary and extra-constitutional actions must be properly made and recognised. The former can only be maintained as long as it does not interfere with the latter. The government has declared a statewide lockdown in response to the COVID-19 catastrophe, and residents have been placed under virtual house arrest.While there is no doubt that ordering a lockdown is imminent under the current factual situation, the type, length, and scope of the lockdown should be subjected to legal review. What is the significance of this? A lockdown is essentially an all-encompassing edict that restricts a wide range of civil freedoms. The first tier of restrictions in a lockdown include"freedom of movement, freedom to practise any profession, trade, or vocation, and freedom to live in any portion of the country".

The "second layer" of restrictions is the result of instances of excess when enforcing the first, resulting in a blatant "infringement" of the otherwise anonymous "right to life and personal liberty". The fact that the state's capacity "to order a lockdown and people' rights to reject excessive limitations on their civil freedoms are both born out of the same constitution, the holy text, in the words of Justice Rohinton Nariman, makes this examination" of lockdown critical.As a result, the examination is governed by the Indian Constitution. It's worth noting that the National Disaster Management Act of 2005 established restrictions restricting freedom of commerce, activity, and profession.

Notably, these standards do not impose any restrictions on one's ability to roam freely. Citizens' freedom of movement "is restricted through a network of executive orders issued under Section 144 of the Code of Criminal Procedure, 1973", in conjunction with the Home Ministry's addition and the colonial-era Epidemic Diseases Act. It's vital to emphasise at this point that the type of "lockdown differs from jurisdiction to jurisdiction", and is mostly determined by the government's judgement of the country's civic life elements.Italy, for example, enables residents to exercise alone near their homes during the lockdown; "France permits outdoor exercise, strolling within 1 km, and walking the dog"; while the United Kingdom permits any "sort of exercise (walking or bicycling)". I'm not sure "whether India should" enable such "concessions" as well, given judgments heavily influenced by "civic" conduct, as well as a variety of other considerations.The main source of these limits is "Article 19(5) of the Constitution, and the essential premise of such limits is a concern for wide public interest".[xxii]

"In the area of constitutional law, there is a well-established contrast between the presence" of power to impose "limits" and the proportionality of those limits.In the present chapter, our examination revolves around this distinction. I studied the limits "in light of their influence or effect on two types of people - traders (right to trade) and migrant workers" - while assessing their proportionality (right to movement). In a society with such wide socioeconomic disparities, broad blanket bans might have severely inequitable enforcement consequences.

Various state governments "have ordered mid-level industry and factory owners to ensure that workers be paid on schedule and in full, even if their activities are completely shut down". The impact of this limitation on trade freedom is twofold: "activities will be halted, and employees will be required to be paid on time". The motivation behind this decree is evident (and admirable), but the long-term impact on the economic interests of a corporation that has already closed might be questioned as inequitable.

Such a guideline "might be traced back to the Constitution's Directive Principles of State Policy". "Article 38", for example, directs "the state to maintain a social order" in which disparities in wealth, position, and opportunity are minimised. Article 38, on the other hand, provides advice for government acts rather than individual initiatives. As a result, the query that arises is whether, in the name of an endemic, the state can shift the duty of ensuring specific "economic interests for one class of citizens to another".

"Enforcing such a directive in the guise of reasonable constraints in the public interest would effectively elevate the issue from Directive Principles of State Policy" to basic citizen responsibilities. In other words, it would be an indirect manner of enforcing basic responsibilities on citizens that would otherwise be unenforceable. A directive like this effectively places the burden of "securing a social order" on citizens (in our instance, traders) and appears to be a cryptic way of enforcing the basic responsibility to "render national service when called upon by the state".One may "argue that morality does not taint such a metric negatively since citizens should have no motivation to shirk their moral obligations" to one another in times of crises. However, the difficulty is "that such a course of action is not contemplated by the Constitution". Certain executive orders cannot require persons to fulfil economic tasks for other citizens in the absence of a law.

"Restrictions under Article 19(5) might reasonably require citizens to desist from trading operations in the public interest", but imposing affirmative responsibilities on persons in the absence of a legislation would be unreasonable. "Even if I look at it through the lens of morality, such civic obligations should be left to the people' choice and cannot be enforced by relying on Article 19(5) stating an abstract broad public interest".To summarise, the "above-mentioned directives go beyond the permissible area under Article 19(5) and might be considered unreasonable to that extent". "Migrant workers are another another group" of residents who are suffering inequitably as a result of the lockdown. The proportionality of restrictive measures principle is founded on the knowledge that a single "uniform formula does not apply to all situations or all persons at all times".

"It is thus because natural circumstances in a community" have positioned persons on various rungs of the ladder, with varying degrees of liberty. If the degree of liberty differs amongst citizens, so will the impact of limitations. To say the least, unintelligent limits put all at once on distinctively positioned persons without taking into consideration their uneven placement in society is a classic example of unfair limits.

"The spectacle of migrant labourers being labelledenemy of lockdown" was witnessed by the entire country. We overlooked the fact that, behind the spectacle, a group of citizens was being automatically converted into offenders of a slew of statutes due to excessive limitations put incomprehensibly on them.The term "unintelligibly" refers to the fact that limitations with such a large economic impact on persons should be considered in light of their socioeconomic level. Because even following the "law becomes a luxury not everyone can afford in these times, it is their social position that dictates their behaviour in the face of limits".[xxiii]

In a society that is profoundly"divided in economic and social terms, the quality of rights, the desirability of restrictions, and the impact of restrictions on citizens will never be the same, and this fundamental feature of our society" places an additional burden on the state to ensure proportionality standards.The imposition of broad limitations may lead to the labelling of one group as lawbreakers purely because of their socioeconomic status. In times of crisis, when "public health concerns loom large, it is all the more important to ensure that the law does not take a back seat, because state-citizen interaction is more intimate in such times, and, needless to say", the Constitution must always register its intervention whenever state and citizens interact.

CONCLUSION

The Government of India has the legal authority to impose lockdown and quarantine, but it lacks constitutional spirit. The legitimacy of the state's coercive activities "under the Epidemic Diseases Act goes against the basic concept of democracy". "There is a need for appropriate laws to cope with health emergencies" caused by epidemics and pandemics such as COVID-19.Such law must include procedural checks in the use of authority by state officers, as well as the notion of state responsibility. People's rights must be effectively balanced with the state's responsibility to preserve people's health. As a result, as "the Supreme Court of India has stated in many judgments, a harmonic structure of Parts III and IV of the Indian Constitution" is the best answer.

While the nation is in the intermediate of an unparalleled catastrophe, the public health emergency necessitates a response that prioritises preserving lives. In these extraordinary circumstances, there is no other option but to enact extraordinary measures, such as a nationwide lockdown, in which it becomes necessary to restrict basic fundamental rights guaranteed by the constitution and deduced by judicial activism in order to mitigate the pandemic's unintended consequences. The truth we are witnessing now is far more shocking than a work of fiction. "Fundamental rights are the most fundamental human rights, whose existence is only validated by the constitution".

Author's Bio

I, Rahul Sharma, Assistant professor, vivekananda college of Law, Aligarh, is going to be publish my research paper on covid-19 and its effects on fundamental rights which gives you more knowledge regarding its impact on fundamental rights under indian constitution.

CHAPTER FOUR

JUVENILE JUSTICE IN INDIA

Author: Rishabh Kumar Jain, pursuing B.B.A.,LL.B.(Hons.) from Christ University

Abstract

To contain the problem of juvenile delinquency in India, the Act pertaining to Juvenile Delinquency has been amended and now trial of juveniles involved in heinous crimes is held as adults There is a trend of increase in juvenile crimes world-over, with more and more involvement of the youth in violent crimes. Indian legal system and judiciary has responded to these trends and has brought some amendments in the laws pertaining to juvenile justice in India.

Introduction

However, for some types of crime, there are older peak ages, and they decline relatively more gradually. Juvenile crimes have become such common phenomena that they raise serious concern in any nation. Under the Indian Laws, Section 2 (k) of the Juvenile Justice (Care and Protection of Children) Act, 2015 (referred generally as JJ Act) juvenile is a person who is below 16 years. Prior to JJ Act of 2015, the age bar for juveniles was 18 years (Juvenile Justice (Care and Protection of Children) Act, 2000, 2006, 2012). The general observation is that criminality/ delinquency peaks in adolescence and diminishes with age, This pattern of crime common across historical, geographical and cultural contexts. There occurs to be a very strong relationship of crime/deviance with age- according to Hirschi and Gottfredson (1983), the age- crime relationship is universal. A juvenile delinquent may be regarded as a child who has allegedly committed/ violated some law, under which his/her act of commission or omission becomes an offense. In common terminology, juvenile is a child who has not attained a certain age at which he can think rationally and often understand the consequences of his/ her act. These children across the world develop at different rates and develop different world- views. They also develop strong romantic/ sexual ideas, and tend to show indulgence in Love and long- term relationships. In fact, the age of the juvenile under the Indian legislations has taken variation in temporal and spatial perspectives. They develop the ability to indulge in long-term – planning and goal setting. Problems arise when these juveniles develop delinquent tendencies, and get into law and order problems.

Research Issues Covered

To understand the latest trends in juvenile delinquency, statistical data from National Crime Records Bureau (official site for data on crimes in India) has been taken and analyzed. Empirical study of juvenile delinquency through visits to Juvenile Homes and Juvenile Boards (Courts) is proposed by the author in the coming years to get a deeper insight into the problem. It aims to delve into some of the causes/reasons for juvenile delinquency and the theoretical prepositions given by different scholars to understand the problem. Further, this data has been linked with the latest amendments made in the Juvenile Justice Act.

Reasons for Juvenile Crimes

Social Factors

Sometimes, the juveniles develop delinquent sub- culture due to cultural deprivation and status frustration that they go through (Albert Cohen, 1955). Delinquent sub- culture theory has been applied in latest studies in the United States (Ling Ren, Hangowel Zhang et al, 2016), where new area of attitude of the juvenile towards the Police in China has been focused. According to Walter B. Miller (1958), some youth (usually belonging to lower class) turn the mainstream culture up- side down, thus whatever is valued and is regarded as positive generally by the is society given up by these youth, and is replaced by just the opposite value system.

Psychological Factors

There are psychological explanations to delinquency also, which can be well understood through Freudian concepts of id, ego and superego. The study indicates that when the neighborhood ties are weak and the social organization factors are not effective, the social control over the members of the society becomes weak, thus leading to delinquent tendencies. Interdisciplinary studies on juvenile delinquency reveal that across the world, many behavioral changes occur in the juveniles/ adolescents, which are related to the sudden changes in their body due hormonal surge, associated with puberty. Sometimes when the self- control and social control through primary groups becomes weak, the juveniles develop delinquent tendencies. Other studies indicate that social factors such as poverty and low education are also responsible for juvenile delinquency (Ombato, John Onyango et al 2013). When the id (the instinctive element of an individual's personality) becomes too strong, and the super- ego becomes weak (the socially taught element of personality) the ego develops into an anti- social person (K. S. Williams 2012). Amongst these neighborhood ties and social organization can be important determinants in the delinquent behavior of the juvenile. The report indicates that the juvenile who receive less familial supervision, or who live in dysfunctional family settings or in disadvantaged families have more chances of getting involved in delinquent behavior. Cloward and Ohlin (1960) feel that juveniles develop different delinquent tendencies depending upon what opportunities are available in their surroundings. The changes are most apparent in physical parameters, such as change in height and weight of the adolescents, and are soon followed by other sexual and physical changes of maturity. David Brandt (2006) has extensively talked about the social and psychological factors responsible for delinquency in India. Study of female inmates in Bangladesh showed a very high incidence of psychiatric disorder among the offenders of Female Juvenile Center (Maruf et al, 2015). Thus, if certain morals are upheld by society, juvenile delinquents give up these values and try to excel in the areas of toughness, over- smarting the others and indulge in things that give them excitement (defined as focal concerns by Miller). Along with the weak neighborhood, ineffective parenting and association of the youth with deviant peers leads to higher rates of offending.

Relevance of Socio- Psychological Studies

Consisting of 54 articles, it sets out children's rights and sets out children's rights and how governments should work together to protect these rights. The United Nations Convention on Rights of Child (CRC) was laid down in 1989, which became a landmark in the international Human Rights legislations. All these researches done in the area of juvenile delinquency under various academic disciplines created the need for a strong instrument at international level that could lay down guidelines for various countries to deal with the situation. The CRC is a legally binding agreement that sets out the civil, political, economic, social and cultural rights of every child, irrespective of their race, religion or abilities. This rights approach shielded in the CRC entailed changes in the area of social; justice, equity and empowerment of the young members of society. India ratified to the CRC in 1992 and since then it has been bringing out various legislation to cover the rights of children.

<u>Evolution of Juvenile Justice Legislations in India</u>

Under the Apprentice Act (1850), it was held that destitute or petty offenders in the age group of 10 and 18 years should be dealt with separately- the convicted children were required to work as apprentices for businessmen. After India got independence, Juvenile Justice policy in India got structured around the mandates prescribed under various articles of Indian constitution (Article 15 (3), 21, 24, 39 (e) & (f), 45 & 47). The important law for neglected and delinquent children in India was passed Central Child's Act (1960), which prohibited imprisonment of children under any circumstances. Prior to coming of British in India, the actions of children were governed under existing Hindu and Muslim laws, where the respective families of the person concerned were held responsible for monitoring the actions of their children. The Juvenile Justice Act, apart for providing for care, protection, rehabilitation and development needs also makes the juvenile adjudication and disposition system child – friendly. The children between 7 and 12 years of age were considered to have sufficient maturity to understand the nature of their actions under certain circumstances. The Act also made provisions for the infrastructure and machinery for care, protection and rehabilitation of children. Some specific laws were passed between 1850 and 1919, like the Apprentice Act (1850), the Code of Criminal Procedure (1861) and the Reformatory School Act (1876 and 1897). In 1986, the central government of India passed a central Act, called the Juvenile Justice Act of 1986. The Code of Criminal Procedure of 1861 allowed for separate trials of persons younger than age 15 and their treatment under the reformatories rather than prisons. However, certain provinces came up with their own legislations to deal with juvenile delinquency (like Bombay, Madras and Pondicherry). New Act dealing with Juvenile delinquency came in 2015, about which a discussion will be held later in this article. Such attempts marked the changing attitude and approach of state to juvenile delinquents, and the transition from penal to reformative philosophy. In this regard, the Reformatory School Act 1876 and 1897 came as a harbinger of such legislation. It declared children's courts and the child welfare board to be two important bodies that would deal with such children. It created juvenile courts for the offenders and juvenile welfare boards for the non- offenders/ neglected children. It was a social legislation that aimed to provide care, protection, treatment and rehabilitation for delinquent and neglected children.

Author's Bio

Rishabh is a first year law student at Christ University Delhi NCR. He is a very determined and ambitious student with a billion dollar dreams in eyes and to make a huge impact in the law field. He has a keen interest in corporate law. Rishabh enjoys both extra circular and circular activities and is very ambitious. He is also a finalist in moot court competition.

DESTROYED AND IGNORED: FALSE ACCUSATIONS AGAINST A MAN

Author: Lisha Chauhan, IV year of B.A.,LL.B.(Hons.) from Fairfield institute of management and technology affiliated with GGSIPU

Co-author: Vibhuti Sharma, IV year of B.A.,LL.B.(Hons.) from Fairfield institute of management and technology affiliated with GGSIPU

Co-author: Yogita Sharma, IV year of B.A.,LL.B.(Hons.) from Fairfield institute of management and technology affiliated with GGSIPU

<u>ABSTRACT</u>

One of the most controversial debates influencing the debate connected with violence against women is the question about the recurrence of bogus charges of rape. The outcomes show that the arrangement of the cases as bogus/no wrongdoing/unjustifiable by the police is itself incorrect and it destroys the honest figures of false charges. The time spent by the police examining misleading cases hindered them from investing energy in the investigation of genuine offenses. Valuable judicial time is additionally spent in hearing situations where false charges are made and are thusly maltreatment of the course of regulation," The effect of false accusations on psychological well-being, profession and the entire existence of men is beyond salvaging. These men accused of fraudulent incriminations of assault are excluded which drives them to live in dread or resort to suicide. According to a survey, 53.2% rape cases filed between April 2013 to July 2014 are false only 1,287 cases were found to be true, and the remaining 1,464 cases were found to be false. How common are the false rape charges? There's an expression that rape "is an allegation easily to be made and hard to be proved. " There are numerous case laws and consequences of the false rape charges on a person's life which will discuss also what are the causes of such allegations.

INTRODUCTION

'Rape' is a serious intolerable heinous crime. In a country like India, where it happens all too often and with every third woman in this society, it additionally has serious consequences. Like being sentenced to life imprisonment or awful - confronting capital punishment. The punishment for such charges seems more or less befitting for someone who has violated another human body, they are absolutely frightening or totally terrifying for someone who did not commit the crime.

You see, throughout the long term, innocent women have gathered the strength to stand against sexual abuse and raise their voices against predators which took a lot of courage. Then, there have also been women who alleged false charges on men for their own sake, as revenge, or for extortion of money from innocents. In a society such as ours, charges as serious as rape cause the accused to be treated as guilty before their trial even ends. Like several vindictive women who weren't victims of sexual abuse, but pretended to be so and framed innocent men for personal gain, revenge, or mental illness.

We all know that the rape has the ability to scar the mental psyche of the victim, and this trauma stays for years but what if the side changes when a woman put false rape charges against a man he loses his whole personality, cannot face his family, lose his honor, job, all the hard-earned reputation in the society and is stigmatized for life.

The court also said that the false allegations of rape of innocents have the potential to destroy the life and career of the accused. Some of the rape charges are alleged by parents of the unmarried daughter of innocent people just to hide their sexual relationship from the society, as we all know that there are few people who are still living in the 19th century.

It is a trend among women to file false rape cases which are exposed by the Delhi Commission of Women (DCW). The report additionally revealed that between June 2013 and December 2013, the number of cases viewed as false was 525. What's more, in the middle, of January 2014 and July 2014, the number of misleading assault cases was 900. Last year, a Delhi court said that it was "turning into an exceptionally difficult position, by and by a-days, for the courts to separate the genuine assault cases from the false ones" while getting the four of a family charged for the present circumstance. It is very shameful and a matter of intense regret even the sick aged persons are not spared from the fake alleged charges of rape for the extortion of money.

Around 40% of the assault cases disposed of by the police in Haryana somewhere in the range of 2018 and 2020 have been proclaimed "bogus", as indicated by the State Crime Record Bureau data. Among gang-rape incidents, 55 cases (39.6 percent) of the absolute 139 were pronounced bogus in 2018. The comparing figures remained at 80 (51 percent) of 157 in 2019 and 72 (45.3 percent) of 159 in 2020. Allegations regarding offenses such as one under section 376 IPC cannot be made at the drop of a hat- in order to settle personal scores.

<u>MAIN CAUSES FOR FALSE RAPE CHARGES</u>

Women intentionally lie about being a victim of rape or sexual assault. Additionally, besides the fact that they falsely claim to have been victimized. However, they may also go so far as to file a police report for their own benefit. This false report can then progress further to the criminal prosecution of an honest individual in a sexual assault or rape case. There exist some reasons why an individual might falsely report a rape or sexual assault.

Some of the more common ulterior motivations of these false cases are

➢ Revenge is another typical motive for false rape allegations. what may surprise a lot of individuals, however, is the fact that this revenge almost never is in response to being dumped by the accused. the potential reason for these revenge accusations is endless. There are concerns over some women in the society who abuse the legal system set up to protect women, for nefarious purposes. The country has seen a rising menace of false rape cases filed by several women with the motive of revenge from the individual.

➢ Extortion of money from an innocent person is also a motive for such false allegations some women in our country abuse our legal system by putting false allegations in the demand for money and promising to withdraw the charges if he gives them what they want. Recently in Gurugram on December 29, police busted a 'honey trapping' racket and arrested 22-year-old Ayushi Bhatia who confessed to her crime of accusing men of bogus sexual assault charges and extorting money.

➢ Personal Gain is the most common reason nowadays for false allegations against men. Working women in the need of promotions or raises in salary put false charges against the men. There's additionally aremarkable case of a woman who accused her gastroenterologist of performing oral sex on her after a colonoscopy since she resented his refusal to act as an expert witness for her in a lawsuit. She then, at that point, sued the gastroenterologist as well.

➢ Break-up is also a reason why some youth alleged false allegations against men. When a relationship ends, women who have had consensual sex make false accusations of rape under the promise of marriage out of vengefulness, to hurt the man and his reputation. Some women ruefully took a break-up on their ego and decide to ruin the life of an individual by making false allegations.

"What if it's just an angry ex with an agenda to get back at you?" Domestic violence and child custody are also some of the cases in the court where women put false allegations in the need of full custody of their child. The growing tendency of filing rape cases against male relatives in matrimonial disputes becomes an easy way for such women in our society to get what they want.

<u>**GUILTY UNTIL PROVEN INNOCENT?**</u>

"A man is considered guilty until proven innocent and a woman is considered innocent until proven guilty."

We consider this statement as bona fide before the investigation by the police or judgment by the court. The question raised is WHY? Nowadays we are enlightened with a word that is 'gender equality.' If we talk about gender equality then criminals irrespective of any gender should get punishment. There is a Latin expression Eiincumbit probation qui dicit, non qui negatwhich states proof lies on him who asserts not on him who denies. This principle has been adopted as a human right under the UN's Universal Declaration of Human Rights, Article 11. It has been perceived as a legal right in countries such as France, Canada, Iran, Italy, Russia, and many more. There is also a guideline known as the presumption of innocence which means an individual is accepted as an innocent until proven guilty. In particular, the presumption of innocence secures the right of a person by not letting him be wrongfully sentenced. The accused is able to prove his innocence in a court of law.

Whereas in India, a man is abused, harassed, blamed and many times tortured by law, police, media, and society as 'guilty' until he proves his innocence. Immediately after the complaint of rape is filed at the police station, the accused is arrested under section 375 of The Indian Penal Code. While the man immediately faces the consequence even if it is a false accusation why no action is taken against the woman who makes those false accusations.

It is also said that the time consumed by police investigating false cases hinders them from spending time investigating serious offenses which as a result leads to faulty investigations. Important judicial time is also spent in hearing situations where bogus charges are made and is consequently an abuse of the process of law. In this way, individuals who make such bogus claims of assault can't be allowed to go scot-free.

As per the National Crime Records Bureau, an aggregate of 38947 assault cases were reported in India in 2016. In 10068-about a fourth of the women claim it was an assault on the bogus promise of marriage. In Andhra Pradesh state, 45% of all rape cases filed in the past two years fell into the false marriage category.

In many cases, women come to an agreement to withdraw the case in exchange for money. I ask myself if they really have been raped, instead of justice why do they yearn for money?

MEDIA AND SOCIETY (MIS)REPRESENTATION

Media and Society both have a narrow coverage related to "Sexual Violence" against men as they focus more on Female victims. The media portrays gender-based sexual violence, showing inadequate depictions and gender stereotypes. Most people think that sexual violence could only be done to females, however, this is an incomplete image showing only one side, as crimes against men are committed in the society itself.

According to the Media and society, only a man can be an abuser, he cannot be a victim in a rape case. These gender stereotypes provoke empathy and create a feeling amongst men which prevents them from attaining their justice. We hear many cases of rape and domestic and sexual violence in media but none of them is related to a man, mostly all of them are related to a woman. Likewise, there are numerous laws made in India to protect women from sexual violence but where is the right of men?

We talk about gender equality, but if a man is a rape victim, we would think it is a bluff or we would not believe that men are also subjected to sexual violence. In an interview with India Times, an international human rights lawyer and activist Vrinda Grover said that "There are no instances of women raping men. I don't think men are facing sexual violence issues as women" this statement is not at all about the gender equality, it is true crime related to women are way much more than as men but crimes related to men cannot be neglected.

Society should start focusing on gender equality, a society needs to let go of the fact that rape and sexual violence could only be done by a man as because of this particular thinking most of the male victims remain unreported.

The media is considered a pillar of society, by giving society accurate news. Thus, media portrayal related to sexual violence can really contribute to society's norms and attitudes.

<u>CONSEQUENCES OF FALSE RAPE ACCUSATIONS</u>

Although accusations of rape or other sexual violence should never take moderately. But the problem is that too many people use these false rape accusations for their own benefit. This false accusation can cause serious consequences. If a person is falsely accused, the results can have tragic impacts on both the person accused as well as the complainant.

- REPUTATION OF A PERSON

A man who is falsely accused in a rape case may never recover from his damaged reputation. If a rape case proved the accused innocent but still, he may never recover from the fact that the accuser does to the reputation of the accused. This means an accused may have to face this consequence their entire life even if it is a lie.

- SELF–ESTEEM

As well as the self-esteem of a person who is being falsely accused in a rape case had been negatively impacted. No matter what every person has their self-esteem and in cases where a man has to deal with being falsely accused, he may never recover from this. It is a serious concern because the falsely accused person may have to face this lifetime.

- MONETARY LOSSES

A person who is falsely accused in a rape case, may have monetary losses, for instances if an accused is working and due to this false allegation, he may have to leave his job or he may get suspended from his job, and they are losing their work over this false allegation which maybe not true. Likewise, their colleagues will judge the accused, they often have the assumption that he is an accused.

- WASTAGE OF TIME

If a person is falsely charged as an accused, then he may have to spend most of the time in a courtroom over something which is not entirely true. For instance, in a false rape case and, in a courtroom, it is decided that a crime is committed by the accused, then the accused who is being falsely charged in a rape case end up going to prison on the statement of an accuser which isn't true, this is an entire wastage of jury time as well as the accused time.

- POLICE TIME

Police do this entire investigation in a rape case but what if a person is falsely accused in a rape case, then this all-determined investigation is nothing but a waste of police timing. Many victims file false accusations on an accused to cause damage to the accused but these types of cases have a serious impact on both the accused and the victim of the case.

- INTERPERSONAL RELATIONSHIPS

The consequence of all this will cause a shattered relationship of an accused with his family and friends to being arrested for the false accusations. The false accusations of an accused will impact his and his family's lives on a deep level. A man who is falsely accused will go through this rest of his life.

Note: In India, if any woman is alleged the individual against false rape charges and extort money can be booked for Section 384 of the IPC and Section 389 (attempts to put any person in fear of an accusation). Not only this but conspiring any criminal conspiracy against a person comes under IPC Section 120B or Section 506 (criminal intimidation) of the Indian Penal Code and taken into judicial custody.

CASE LAWS

Vishnu Tiwari vs state of UP: In this case, the accused Vishnu Tiwari was taken into custody for the first time in September 2000, when an FIR was lodged by a woman, her husband, and her father-in-law. The complainants were from the same village. He was falsely charged with sexually assaulting, raping, and beating her when she was five months pregnant. According to Vishnu Tiwari, the complainant has accused him in order to take revenge There was a land and animal dispute between the above mentioned. He never met the woman and just knew her as a daughter-in-law. They just wanted the money through the Harijan act. He attained bail but was arrested again in 2001. He was sentenced to life imprisonment in 2003 after being found guilty under sections 3(1)(7) and 3(2)(5) of the SC/ST Atrocities Act.

He challenged this judgment by a trial court in 2005 but his petition was accounted defective as the required documents were not in place. It remained this way for 16 years. After 16 years, he was proven innocent. Just for the sake of revenge and greediness, an innocent had to suffer in jail for 20 years for a crime he never committed. His ancestral lands also had to be discharged to pay lawyers. While he was in prison, his parents and his two brothers died and he couldn't even attend their last rites. Many times, he felt that he should just die. After returning from jail in January 2021, he found his house empty and his family was gone. He left jail with only Rs. 600 which was handed over to him by the jail administration. That is all he has to rebuild his life.

Indore case 2021: In January 2021, a 19-year-old girl told the police that she was kidnapped, raped, and stabbed by 5 men. She told that they put her in a jute bag and outlined to throw her on the railway tracks. However, when the investigation started, it was found the teenager's claims were incompatible and baseless. No evidence was found to support her claim and her claims were false and fabricated. The complainant even went to the lengths of stabbing herself to prove her story.Later, the Indore police decided to book the girl under 182/211, IPC for filing a false case.

Satara case 2019: A woman in the Satara district of Maharashtra accused two men of raping her in a car. According to her, they promised her a job in exchange. However, the charge was false and fabricated. While investigating, it was found out that one of the men was out of the country while the other was not in Satara but in Pune on the day she claimed to have been raped. Apparently, the woman filed the bogus case only to tarnish the reputation of the men.

Ghaziabad case 2017: A minor daughter was provoked by her maternal uncle to accuse her own father of raping her. The father who was accused of the crime spent three long years in jail for a crime he never committed. During the first trial, the story started to fall apart and the daughter accepted that she fabricated the false case. She admitted that she did this under the influence of her maternal uncle. The uncle on the other hand was only imprisoned for one month and charged a fine of Rs. 50,000.

Chennai false rape case 2010: An engineering student, Santosh residing in Chennai, was accused of raping a girl and impregnating her after the two families were supposed to get their kids married to each other, had a fall out due to a dispute regarding the property. The girl's mother claimed that the boy had impregnated her daughter and refused to marry her. But he denied any such relationship with her. After being denied, she and her parents lodged a complaint of rape and the boy was arrested.

In February 2010, he came out on bail, and by that time the girl had delivered the baby. They took a DNA test on the baby and it proved that Santosh was not the father. Santosh filed a suit for damages as this case ruined his career and life as he was an engineering student and the case cost him Rs. 2 lakhs. A Chennai court offered him Rs. 15 lakhs as compensation. Despite being innocent, he spent 7 years in jail.

#Mentoo

Women have fought a long battle for their rights in the country.This long battle was fought so that women can get justice and respect in society. Earlier, women and their families were too afraid and embarrassed to step forward and file a complaint against rape. They thought"what will society think about them?", "How will society treat them?", "They will be portrayed as characterless", and "No man will marry them."But the situation has drastically changed after the 2013 amendment.After the Nirbhaya Rape case, in 2012, the Criminal Law Amendment bill overturned our rape and sexual assault laws in 2013.

A social movement (#metoo) has also helped women to come forward and raise their voices against the sexual assault or harassment they have been through. Reportedly, some women have also taken advantage of #metoo and made false accusations against men.As we all are aware of the phrase "keep yourself in my shoes" sowhat about those women who actually are the victim of sexual assault and sexual harassment? The sentiments of those women are ignored by those who make false accusations and are only greedy for their own good. There are several cases in which the victim has actually suffered rape, their cases are still pending in the court for many years. They are yet to get justice.While we know what punishment awaits him if he is found guilty of this crime, we don't know what will happen if he is found innocent. Who will give him the dignity and reputation he lost? No one!

Now is the time to overturn the criminal justice system as well. Not only for women but also for men.

CONCLUSION

Being wrongfully accused of criminal offenses can lead to seriously negative and unfavorableconsequences for those wrongfully accused and their families. Our Indian society and our media concentrate extensively on women's incidents of abuse about their safety only. So, when a man is harassed with wrong charges on him, what about that? The ongoing legal framework is inefficient in preventing bogus rape charges and in protecting the accused from being wrongfully detained as well as criticized. Even if one innocent is acquitted, one cannot regain that status. The wrongfully accused may lose their reputation, sense of self-worth, respect, their place in the community, their career, their friends, partners, and sometimes their freedom. You can't prove your innocence to every single individual. People are quick to judge a rape case without even knowing whether the person is guilty or not that is because we really want severe regulations for the misleading assault cases in India which can save innocent.

Authors' Bio

1. This article is written by Lisha Chauhan. She is a 4th-year B.A.LLB student from Fairfield Institute of management and technology affiliated with GGSIPU. Lisha is an avid and passionate writer. She loves to write on legal issues which are happening in society as well as across the globe.

2. This article is written by Vibhuti sharma, a 4th year and a B.A.LLB student from Fairfield Institute of management and technology affiliated with GGSIPU. Vibhuti loves to read and write about various legal issues. She is enthusiastic and passionate about her work.

3. Yogita Sharma has written this article. She is a 4th year B.A.LLB student from Fairfield Institute of management and technology affiliated with GGSIPU. She is an ardent reader and a passionate writer interested in legal as well as creative writing.

CHAPTER SIX

INHERITANCE: RIGHT OF A MUSLIM WOMAN

Author: Yukta Sharma, III year of B.A.,LL.B.(Hons.) from REVA University, Bengaluru

"Despite the facts that around half of the world's population is acquired by the women and the significant contributions made by them in economic, social and political areas, they are denied to inherit their deceased parents' property"[1].

INTRODUCTION

The Muslims does not acknowledge the concept of "inheritance by birth"[2]. The property can only be inherited after the death of a person and not when he alive[3]. The two genders maybe equal in the law of legacy but it's not the case in Islam. Due to the customary laws and patriarchal mind-set, the infant daughters, in ancient Islamic societies, were slaughtered out of the fear of inheritance of the property (family's wealth). The period was known as Jahiliyyah[4] and during that era women were not regarded as the heirs to their parents' estate[5]. At that time it was usual that the ones who ride horse or know to fight the battle can only have the right of inheritance and there was no tradition of inheritance to females. According to Iman-al-Tabari, women and children were not entitled to take any share for inheritance in the property. To overcome the same expression, Quran allows the women to inherit their share in the virtue of these verses.

INHERITANCE RIGHTS OF MUSLIM FEMALE IN QURAN

The Quran states that a mother, wife, widow and daughters are entitled for inheritance and provides some rights to them which are mentioned in verses 7 and 33 of Surah-al-Nisa. Verses 11 and 12 of the Surah provide comprehensive guidelines of inheritance of property and how it would be allocated according to Qur'anic procedures. When it comes to inheritance the share of the man is twofold from that of the woman. Women are deemed inferior as that of their male counterparts[6] and this is known as Nafaqah[7]. Also there is an additional responsibility on man to pay Mehr[8]; which is considered as a token of love and dignity provided by the husband to his wife, agreed at the time of marriage as a future security. So, a mehr automatically comprises a woman's property which she may utilize whenever and however she needs.

DIVISION OF SHARE: SHARIAT LAW

Unlike Hindu law, the division of share is already fixed under Muslim law. There is a fixed proportionate of share division. It is believed that a man has additional responsibilities to look after, maintain and fulfil their needs, also a woman is also maintained by her husband but her brothers are only dependant on ancestral property, thus a Muslim man is entitled for twofold of the share than that of a Muslim female. There are certain rules for the same in different scenarios:

1. SHARE OF DAUGHTER

A son is entitled to take double share as that of daughter. Where there is no brother she is entitled to take half share from the total property. She is considered as the absolute owner of the property or share she receives and she is legally entitled to manage, control and dispose it off as per her wishes and needs[9].

2. SHARE OF WIFE

In case of death of the husband a widow is entitled to get one-eighth share when there are children and in case where there are no children she will get one-fourth share. And if there is more than one wife, the share will decrease to one-sixteenth[10].

3. SHARE OF MOTHER

A muslin woman, being a mother is entitled to get one-sixth of the share from her son's property if he is a father as well. And when there are no grandchildren she will get one-third of the share[11].

RIGHT TO MEHR: SPECIFICALLY

Mehr is also known as dower. It is the right to a Muslim woman provided by the Quran. And the Verses 4 of Sura-ul-Nisa provides the right to Muslim woman to claim their dower. Mehr is paid by the husband to his wife, either at the time of marriage or anytime during the marriage or at the time of dissolution of marriage[12]. He has the right to increase the dower, at any time after the marriage but no right to decrease the dower[13]. And he may willingly give his entire property as mehr to his wife.

The objective behind paying the Mehr is:

- It acts as a prestige of Muslim marriage.
- Token of respect
- To provide substance to marriage
- To keep a check on husband's power to give divorce
- To curb the practice of bigamy

The mehr is considered as the absolute property of a Muslim woman and can be used by her as per her want and need. It acts as a future security for her. Denial to pay mehr can result into non fulfilment of marital obligations from the woman's part[14].

CONCLUSION

In the matter of inheritance of property the Muslim women are getting comparatively less share than their male counterparts. And there are various reasons and responsibilities which are covered in the above paragraphs. Though the early Islamic society has not a systematic and equal manner of distribution of property and the female heirs were discriminated but later when Quran came, it has given the rights to Muslim females as well to inherit the family property.

Looking into the current situation the female, though getting less share than their male counterparts but possess a right to Mehr by their husbands, which is a compulsory practice under Muslim law. Such a variety of practices differentiate the ways of inheritance in Muslim law to that of in Hindu law.

Author's Bio

This paper is written by Yukta Sharma, a second-year Law student at REVA University, Bengaluru. She has done her previous research on Gender Sensitization, Marital Rape and other social issues, with special reference to women as an area of study. She is interested in content writing and research analysis in respect of various social issues